KNOW YOUR GOVERNMENT

The
U.S. Mint

The U.S. Mint

Paul Wolman

CHELSEA HOUSE PUBLISHERS
New York • Philadelphia

3   5   7   9   8   6   4

Library of Congress Cataloging-in-Publication Data

Wolman, Paul
  The United States Mint.
  (Know your government)
  Bibliography: p. 89
  Includes index.
  1. United States. Bureau of the Mint—History.
  2. Mints—United States—History. 3. Coinage—United States—History.
I. Title   II. Series: Know your government (New York, N.Y.)
HG459.W65   1987   353.0082'2   86-31720

ISBN 0-87754-829-3
      0-7910-0879-7 (pbk.)

Project Editor: Nancy Priff
Book Editor: Rafaela Ellis
Associate Editor: Linda Fridy
Art Director: Maureen McCafferty
Series Designer: Anita Noble
Chief Copy Editor: Melissa R. Padovani
Project Coordinator: Kathleen P. Luczak
Production Manager: Brian Shulik

ABOUT THE COVER

The United States Mint produces coins for the nation. The gold piece on the
cover is an artistic example of the mint's work and its image reflects the
nation's ideals. The coin shows a woman striding forward with a torch and an
olive branch. The woman represents Liberty, a symbol of American
independence. Her torch lights the way for the nation and her olive branch
symbolizes peace.

CONTENTS

Introduction 7

1 A Revolutionary Idea......................... 17

2 American Money: From Wampum to Washington... 21

3 Development of the Mint and Coinage 33

4 The Mint Branches Out 41

5 The Civil War and the Battle of the Standards..... 47

6 The United States as a World Money Power 57

7 Today's Mint—People and Powers............... 65

8 Today's Mint at Work 75

9 New Challenges 85

Glossary....................................... 88

Selected References 89

Index 90

KNOW YOUR GOVERNMENT

The American Red Cross
The Bureau of Indian Affairs
The Centers for Disease Control
The Central Intelligence Agency
The Children, Youth, and
  Families Division
The Department of Agriculture
The Department of the Air Force
The Department of the Army
The Department of Commerce
The Department of Defense
The Department of Education
The Department of Energy
The Department of Health
  and Human Services
The Department of Housing
  and Urban Development
The Department of the Interior
The Department of Justice
The Department of Labor
The Department of the Navy
The Department of State
The Department of
  Transportation
The Department of the Treasury
The Drug Enforcement
  Administration
The Environmental
  Protection Agency
The Equal Opportunities
  Commission
The Federal Aviation
  Administration
The Federal Bureau of
  Investigation
The Federal Communications
  Commission
The Federal Election Commission

The Federal Railroad
  Administration
The Food and Drug
  Administration
The Food and Nutrition Division
The House of Representatives
The Immigration and
  Naturalization Service
The Internal Revenue Service
The Interstate Commerce
  Commission
The National Foundation on the
  Arts and Humanities
The National Park Service
The National Science Foundation
The Presidency
The Securities and
  Exchange Commission
The Selective Service System
The Senate
The Small Business
  Administration
The Smithsonian
The Supreme Court
The Tennessee Valley Authority
The U.S. Information Agency
The U.S. Arms Control and
  Disarmament Agency
The U.S. Coast Guard
The U.S. Commission on
  Civil Rights
The U.S. Fish and Wildlife Service
The U.S. Mint
The U.S. Nuclear Regulatory
  Commission
The U.S. Postal Service
The U.S. Secret Service
The Veterans Administration

INTRODUCTION

Government: Crises of Confidence

Arthur M. Schlesinger, jr.

From the start, Americans have regarded their government with a mixture of reliance and mistrust. The men who founded the republic did not doubt the indispensability of government. "If men were angels," observed the 51st Federalist Paper, "no government would be necessary." But men are not angels. Since human beings are subject to wicked as well as to noble impulses, government was deemed essential to assure freedom and order.

At the same time, the American revolutionaries knew that government could also become a source of injury and oppression. The men who gathered in Philadelphia in 1787 to write the Constitution therefore had two purposes in mind. They wanted to establish a strong central authority and to limit that central authority's capacity to abuse its power.

To prevent the abuse of power, the founding fathers wrote two basic principles into the new Constitution. The principle of federalism divided power between the state governments and the central authority. The principle of the separation of powers subdivided the central authority itself into three branches—the executive, the legislative, and the judiciary—so that "each may be a check on the other." The *Know Your Government* series focuses on the major executive departments and agencies in these branches of the federal government.

The Constitution did not plan the executive branch in any detail. After vesting the executive power in the president, it assumed the existence of "executive departments" without specifying what these departments should be. Congress began defining their functions in 1789 by creating the Departments of State, Treasury, and War. The secretaries in charge of these departments made up President Washington's first cabinet. Congress also provided for a legal officer, and President Washington soon invited the attorney general, as he was called, to attend cabinet meetings. As need required, Congress created more executive departments.

Setting up the cabinet was only the first step in organizing the American state. With almost no guidance from the Constitution, President Washington, seconded by Alexander Hamilton, his brilliant secretary of the treasury, equipped the infant republic with a working administrative structure. The Federalists believed in both executive energy and executive accountability and set high standards for public appointments. The Jeffersonian opposition had less faith in strong government and preferred local government to the central authority. But when Jefferson himself became president in 1801, although he set out to change the direction of policy, he found no reason to alter the framework the Federalists had erected.

By 1801 there were about 3,000 federal civilian employees in a nation of a little more than 5 million people. Growth in territory and population steadily enlarged national responsibilities. Thirty years later, when Jackson was president, there were more than 11,000 government workers in a nation of 13 million.

The federal establishment was increasing at a faster rate than the population.

Jackson's presidency brought significant changes in the federal service. He believed that the executive branch contained too many officials who saw their jobs as "species of property" and as "a means of promoting individual interest." Against the idea of a permanent service based on life tenure, Jackson argued for the periodic redistribution of federal offices, contending that this was the democratic way and that official duties could be made "so plain and simple that men of intelligence may readily qualify themselves for their performance." He called this policy rotation-in-office. His opponents called it the spoils system.

In fact, partisan legend exaggerated the extent of Jackson's removals. More than 80 percent of federal officeholders retained their jobs. Jackson discharged no larger a proportion of government workers than Jefferson had done a generation earlier. But the rise in these years of mass political parties gave federal patronage new importance as a means of building the party and of rewarding activists. Jackson's successors were less restrained in the distribution of spoils. As the federal establishment grew—to nearly 40,000 by 1861—the politicization of the public service excited increasing concern.

After the Civil War the spoils system became a major political issue. High-minded men condemned it as the root of all political evil. The spoilsmen, said the British commentator James Bryce, "have distorted and depraved the mechanism of politics." Patronage, by giving jobs to unqualified, incompetent, and dishonest persons, lowered the standards of public service and nourished corrupt political machines. Office-seekers pursued presidents and cabinet secretaries without mercy. "Patronage," said Ulysses S. Grant after his presidency, "is the bane of the presidential office." "Every time I appoint someone to office," said another political leader, "I make a hundred enemies and one ingrate." George William Curtis, the president of the National Civil Service Reform League, summed up the indictment. He said,

> The theory which perverts public trusts into party spoils, making public employment dependent upon personal favor and not on proved merit, necessarily ruins the self-respect of public employees, destroys the function of party in a republic, prostitutes elections into a desperate strife for personal profit, and degrades the national character by lowering the moral tone and standard of the country.

The object of civil service reform was to promote efficiency and honesty in the public service and to bring about the ethical regeneration of public life. Over bitter opposition from politicians, the reformers in 1883 passed the Pendleton Act, establishing a bipartisan Civil Service Commission, competitive examinations, and appointment on merit. The Pendleton Act also gave the president authority to extend by executive order the number of "classified" jobs—that is, jobs subject to the merit system. The act applied initially only to about 14,000 of the more than 100,000 federal positions. But by the end of the 19th century 40 percent of federal jobs had moved into the classified category.

Civil service reform was in part a response to the growing complexity of American life. As society grew more organized and problems more technical, official duties were no longer so plain and simple that any person of intelligence could perform them. In public service, as in other areas, the all-round man was yielding ground to the expert, the amateur to the professional. The excesses of the spoils system thus provoked the counter-ideal of scientific public administration, separate from politics and, as far as possible, insulated against it.

The cult of the expert, however, had its own excesses. The idea that administration could be divorced from policy was an illusion. And in the realm of policy, the expert, however much segregated from partisan politics, can never attain perfect objectivity. He remains the prisoner of his own set of values. It is these values rather than technical expertise that determine fundamental judgments of public policy. To turn over such judgments to experts, moreover, would be to abandon democracy itself; for in a democracy final decisions must be made by the people and their elected representatives. "The business of the expert," the British political scientist Harold Laski rightly said, "is to be on tap and not on top."

Politics, however, were deeply ingrained in American folkways. This meant intermittent tension between the presidential government, elected every four years by the people, and the permanent government, which saw presidents come and go while it went on forever. Sometimes the permanent government knew better than its political masters; sometimes it opposed or sabotaged valuable new initiatives. In the end a strong president with effective cabinet secretaries could make the permanent government responsive to presidential purpose, but it was often an exasperating struggle.

The struggle within the executive branch was less important, however, than the growing impatience with bureaucracy in society as a whole. The 20th century saw a considerable expansion of the federal establishment. The Great Depression and the New Deal led the national government to take on a variety of new responsibilities. The New Deal extended the federal regulatory apparatus. By 1940, in a nation of 130 million people, the number of federal workers for the first time passed the 1 million mark. The Second World War brought federal civilian employment to 3.8 million in 1945. With peace, the federal establishment declined to around 2 million by 1950. Then growth resumed, reaching 2.8 million by the 1980s.

The New Deal years saw rising criticism of "big government" and "bureaucracy." Businessmen resented federal regulation. Conservatives worried about the impact of paternalistic government on individual self-reliance, on community responsibility, and on economic and personal freedom. The nation in effect renewed the old debate between Hamilton and Jefferson in the early republic, although with an ironic exchange of positions. For the Hamiltonian constituency, the "rich and well-born," once the advocate of affirmative government, now condemned government intervention, while the Jeffersonian constituency, the plain people, once the advocate of a weak central government and of states' rights, now favored government intervention.

In the 1980s, with the presidency of Ronald Reagan, the debate has burst out with unusual intensity. According to conservatives, government intervention abridges liberty, stifles enterprise, and is inefficient, wasteful, and arbitrary. It disturbs the harmony of the self-adjusting market and creates worse troubles than it solves. Get government off our backs, according to the popular cliché, and our problems will solve themselves. When government is necessary, let it be at the local level, close to the people. Above all, stop the inexorable growth of the federal government.

In fact, for all the talk about the "swollen" and "bloated" bureaucracy, the federal establishment has not been growing as inexorably as many Americans seem to believe. In 1949, it consisted of 2.1 million people. Thirty years later, while the country had grown by 70 million, the federal force had grown only by 750,000. Federal workers were a smaller percentage of the population in 1985 than they were in 1955—or in 1940. The federal establishment, in short, has not kept pace with population growth. Moreover, national defense and the postal service account for 60 percent of federal employment.

Why then the widespread idea about the remorseless growth of government? It is partly because in the 1960s the national government assumed new and intrusive functions:

affirmative action in civil rights, environmental protection, safety and health in the workplace, community organization, legal aid to the poor. Although this enlargement of the federal regulatory role was accompanied by marked growth in the size of government on all levels, the expansion has taken place primarily in state and local government. Whereas the federal force increased by only 27 percent in the 30 years after 1950, the state and local government force increased by an astonishing 212 percent.

Despite the statistics, the conviction flourishes in some minds that the national government is a steadily growing behemoth swallowing up the liberties of the people. The foes of Washington prefer local government, feeling it is closer to the people and therefore allegedly more responsive to popular needs. Obviously there is a great deal to be said for settling local questions locally. But local government is characteristically the government of the locally powerful. Historically, the way the locally powerless have won their human and constitutional rights has often been through appeal to the national government. The national government has vindicated racial justice against local bigotry, defended the Bill of Rights against local vigilantism, and protected natural resources against local greed. It has civilized industry and secured the rights of labor organizations. Had the states' rights creed prevailed, there would perhaps still be slavery in the United States.

The national authority, far from diminishing the individual, has given most Americans more personal dignity and liberty than ever before. The individual freedoms destroyed by the increase in national authority have been in the main the freedom to deny black Americans their rights as citizens; the freedom to put small children to work in mills and immigrants in sweatshops; the freedom to pay starvation wages, require barbarous working hours, and permit squalid working conditions; the freedom to deceive in the sale of goods and securities; the freedom to pollute the environment—all freedoms that, one supposes, a civilized nation can readily do without.

"Statements are made," said President John F. Kennedy in 1963, "labelling the Federal Government an outsider, an intruder, an adversary.... The United States Government is not a stranger or not an enemy. It is the people of fifty states joining in a national effort.... Only a great national effort by a great people working together can explore the mysteries of space, harvest the products at the bottom of the ocean, and mobilize the human, natural, and material resources of our lands."

So an old debate continues. However, Americans are of two minds. When pollsters ask large, spacious questions—Do you think government has become too involved in your lives? Do you think government should stop regulating business?—a sizable majority opposes big government. But when asked specific questions about the practical work of government—Do you favor social security? unemployment compensation? Medicare? health and safety standards in factories? environmental protection? government guarantee of jobs for everyone seeking employment? price and wage controls when inflation threatens?—a sizable majority approves of intervention.

In general, Americans do not want less government. What they want is more efficient government. They want government to do a better job. For a time in the 1970s, with Vietnam and Watergate, Americans lost confidence in the national government. In 1964, more than three-quarters of those polled had thought the national government could be trusted to do right most of the time. By 1980 only one-quarter was prepared to offer such trust. But by 1984 trust in the federal government to manage national affairs had climbed back to 45 percent.

Bureaucracy is a term of abuse. But it is impossible to run any large organization, whether public or private, without a bureaucracy's division of labor and hierarchy of authority. And we live in a world of large organizations. Without bureaucracy modern society would collapse. The problem is not to abolish bureaucracy, but to make it flexible, efficient, and capable of innovation.

Two hundred years after the drafting of the Constitution, Americans still regard government with a mixture of reliance and mistrust—a good combination. Mistrust is the best way to keep government reliable. Informed criticism is the means of correcting governmental inefficiency, incompetence, and arbitrariness; that is, of best enabling government to play its essential role. For without government, we cannot attain the goals of the founding fathers. Without an understanding of government, we cannot have the informed criticism that makes government do the job right. It is the duty of every American citizen to *Know Your Government*—which is what this series is all about.

SEC. OF STATE.

T. JEFFERSON.

Secretary of State Thomas Jefferson directed the first mint of the United States, created in 1792.

ONE

A Revolutionary Idea

The United States Mint and the national currency—like the country itself—were born of revolution. As one of the earliest acts of rebellion, the American colonies began to coin money shortly after they declared their independence from Britain. When the new nation's leaders wrote the Constitution, one of their first acts under its powers was to found a mint—"Ye Olde Mint"—in Philadelphia. And such leaders as Benjamin Franklin, Thomas Jefferson, Alexander Hamilton, and George Washington gave close attention to the nation's coinage.

Why would the country's founders devote so much attention to the establishment and running of a mint? Because, in a time before mass media, coinage advertised the sovereignty, solvency, and standards of a nation. For years, individuals used European coins to buy tobacco in the colonies, sugar in the Indies, slaves in Africa, and silks in Japan. Through these coins, people all over the world became familiar with the faces of Europe's rulers and recognized the wealth and power of those countries.

America's founding fathers wanted to build this same kind of recognition within and beyond their new nation's borders, and they believed that coins could help them do it.

In 1792, they officially founded the first national Mint of the United States and placed it under the control of Thomas Jefferson's State Department. Seven years later, Congress made the mint an independent agency, reporting directly to the president. In 1873, Congress changed the mint's name to the Bureau of the Mint and placed it under the Treasury Department's authority. Most recently, in 1984, this bureau of the Treasury Department was renamed the United States Mint. But its basic mission has remained the same: to produce the United States' circulating coins. (The Bureau of Engraving and Printing produces the nation's paper currency.)

For generations, America's mint and coinage have symbolized the ideals of the nation's founders. Yet they have also changed in reponse to the times, as American society has built and rebuilt itself. In the 1830s, people in the developing regions of the South pressed Congress to construct new branch mints there to express their disagreements with the wealthier states

"Ye Olde Mint" in Philadelphia produced American coins for many years.

18

and banks of the East. During the Civil War, the minting of new coins in the North helped sustain the credibility of the Union cause and Union currency. After the Civil War, the merits of gold and silver coinage became the focus of a political battle between those who supported individual farms and small businesses and those who favored big business. In the 20th century, American coinage and banks have become intimately involved in the maintenance of a complex, worldwide economy. Today, the mint's advanced methods of manufacturing, industrial management, and statistical expertise are far different from the practices of the colonial days. Yet the United States Mint remains a part of the federal government, responsible to Congress and, ultimately, to the people.

Native Americans often bartered with early colonists, using fur pelts, cloth, and other goods instead of money.

TWO

American Money: From Wampum to Washington

In the early years, the new American colonies had an undeveloped money system. Colonists commonly transacted business by barter—the direct exchange of goods or services without the use of money. For instance, if one settler had too many beaver furs but needed an axe, he could trade his furs to a chilly settler who had an extra axe. In situations such as this, the colonists didn't need money. But as the colonies developed, transactions became more complex. If the buyer didn't have furs or other items to trade, he would pay for the axe with money, which the axe seller could use to buy a fur from someone else.

Colonial Money

A common form of money for the early colonists was wampum, strings of purple-and-white beads made from quahog clam shells. First used by Indians, wampum was legal tender (a lawful form of money) in Rhode Island until 1670 and in New York until 1701. However, colonists easily counterfeited wampum from bones, stones, and poor-quality shells. Eventually, colonists found large amounts of quahog clam shells on Long Island and produced wampum in such quantities that it became meaningless as money. Even so, frontier settlers used wampum as small change until the early 1800s.

While the British ruled the early colonies, the primary form of money was British pounds, shillings, and pence. The economic activity of the rapidly growing colonies became so great, however, that the British could not supply enough coinage. Some colonies made their own coins, such as the Massachusetts Bay Colony, which minted Pine Tree Shillings and other coins. Colonists also used other foreign gold and silver coins, including French guineas, Portuguese johannes (or "joes"), and Spanish doubloons.

Spanish coins were especially common in the colonies, because Spanish conquistadors had set up mints in the New World,

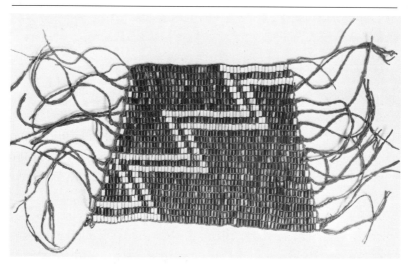

Iroquois Indians wove wampum into armlets (bands worn around the upper arm) that could be traded for valuable goods.

Spanish pillar dollars—the famous "pieces of eight"—supplemented the British currency used in the colonies.

in Mexico City and Lima, Peru, where they had found huge quantities of gold and silver. And pirates and privateers (mercenaries hired by governments to capture and rob enemy ships) brought Spanish coins into the American colonies to purchase supplies and luxury goods. Spanish pillar dollars, especially popular with colonists, depicted two pillars symbolizing the Strait of Gibraltar, through which ships sailed from the Mediterranean to the New World. These silver coins became known as "pieces of eight" because they could be cut into eight pie-shaped "bits" for change: "two bits" equaled 25 cents, "four bits" equaled 50 cents, and so on.

Eventually, counterfeiting and crimes involving coinage became serious problems in the colonies. Because coins contained precious metals, criminals often "clipped" them, shaving off the edges and then melting down the shavings to recoin or sell the metal. In 1768, bands of coin clippers were reputed to be working throughout the colonies, from New Hampshire to North Carolina. As the colonies' relations with Britain became more hostile, clipping the king's coins became a form of revolutionary resistance to the British crown. Although it was hard to convict individuals of clipping, the crime was punishable by death. To discourage clipping, governments began stamping fine parallel ridges on the edges of precious-metal coins—a process known as milling or reeding. Missing or defaced ridges were unmistakable evidence of clipping.

Revolutionary Money

When the colonies rebelled openly, one of their first acts was to demonstrate their independence by issuing their own money. They authorized paper notes as early as May of 1775. In 1776 the Continental Congress issued currency coins made of silver, brass (an alloy, or mixture, of copper and zinc or tin), and pewter (an alloy of tin and lead). These coins depicted a sundial and bore the Latin inscription *Fugio*, meaning "I fly," referring to the rapid passage of time. "Mind Your Business" was another appropriate inscription on coins that depicted a chain of 13 links with the motto "American Congress: We Are One." These may have been the first official coins of the new nation. In 1778, the Articles of Confederation authorized the states to coin money, too, but the Constitution later revoked that right.

Uneven reeding indicated a counterfeit coin (right). Real coins had uniform ridges.

Benjamin Franklin wanted moral mottoes and anti-British propaganda to adorn colonial coins.

Benjamin Franklin, the inventor and publisher, was the American minister to France during the Revolutionary War. He took an early interest in America's coinage. From France, Franklin corresponded secretly with Edward Brigden, an English coiner who was sympathetic to the revolution. Franklin wanted to use moral or economic mottoes on one side of the new coins, such as "A Penny Saved Is a Penny Got," "The Fear of the Lord Is the Beginning of Wisdom," and "Keep Thy Shop and It Will Keep Thee." On the other side of the coins, he wanted to show propaganda, such as scenes of the king's soldiers burning the "defenceless towns of Connecticut," to strengthen public resolve to fight the British. But although Brigden actually sent sample coin designs to Franklin in France, the idea went no further.

Early National Money

One of the many important tasks facing the new nation's leaders was to design a currency system whose value would be known and respected widely. Most governments earned respect for their national money system by using precious-metal coinage.

But America was still fighting for its independence, and the Continental Congress lacked the resources to buy precious metals to make large numbers of coins. After the war, revolutionary leaders proposed different coinage systems based on those in their home states (such as Massachusetts Pine Tree Shillings and New Jersey Cents). During the next ten years, the country's leaders considered three major national coinage plans: the Morris plan, the Jefferson plan, and the Hamilton plan.

Under the Articles of Confederation, Congress asked Robert Morris, the superintendent of finance, to prepare the first national coinage plan. His plan proposed a decimal coinage system, based on multiples of 10, instead of a system based on multiples of 12 (12 pence to a shilling and 240 pence to a pound). Morris commissioned a Philadelphia blacksmith to make sample coins depicting an eye surrounded by rays, with 13 stars and the Latin motto *Nova Constellatio*, or "New Constellation." The stars represented the original 13 states as new and important additions to the political universe. Morris recommended silver as the monetary standard and developed a complicated system for converting coins to the standards used in different states. Because of the plan's complexity—and because Congress was having difficulty raising money for its own operations—the Morris

Before the advent of national currency, states minted their own coins, such as this Pine Tree Shilling from Massachusetts.

Robert Morris proposed a silver standard and a decimal system of coinage.

plan was abandoned. But his argument for a decimal coinage survived and eventually became part of the coinage system.

In June of 1783, Thomas Jefferson became chairman of the Continental Congress Currency Committee. When the war ended, Americans began to send specie (metal of any kind in coin form) out of the United States to purchase goods unavailable during the war, and the need for a good coinage system became urgent. Recognizing this, Jefferson proposed a system with the dollar as the United States monetary unit—similar to the Spanish milled dollar. In 1785, Congress ratified Jefferson's proposals for a ten-dollar gold piece, a silver half-dollar, a double tenth, a twentieth, and a copper hundredth.

Congress also accepted Robert Morris's recommendation for a copper two-hundredth piece (a halfpenny), so that people could pay and be paid in more exact sums. Sample coins, produced according to this system, once again depicted rays sur-

The **Confederatio** *coin was never mass-produced.*

rounding 13 stars. Along with the stars, the motto *Confederatio,* or "Confederation," appeared on the reverse (the "tails" side of a coin). An Indian stepping on a crown—symbolizing the brave New World's rejection of the Old World monarchy—appeared on the obverse (the "heads" side) with a motto emphasizing the point: *Inimica Tyrannis America*—"America hates tyrants." Unfortunately, the young nation lacked the facilities for mass production of these coins.

While plans for a national coinage paused, the Constitution was ratified in 1788, and George Washington became the nation's first president in 1789. One of Washington's first actions in office was to appoint a cabinet of assistants to carry out the specific functions of the executive branch of the government— including a secretary of the treasury to help control the nation's finances.

In 1789, Washington appointed Alexander Hamilton as the first secretary of the treasury. Hamilton, who believed in a strong national government run by the "rich and well-born," wanted merchants and government officials to design and administer the nation's new currency system. He pointed to Article 1, section 8 of the Constitution, which gives Congress the power "to coin money, regulate the Value thereof, and of foreign Coin," and "to provide for the Punishment of counterfeiting." Hamilton persuaded Congress to establish a federal bank (the First Bank of the United States) to manage federal money and supervise the activities of local banks.

Hamilton also called for the creation of a mint and a workable coinage system, managed and supported by the federal government. In 1791, he submitted a report outlining his ideas—the basis for the present American mint system. In his report, Hamilton concluded that the best unit for American coinage was the dollar, that the dollar should be based on the decimal system, and that the fineness (precious metal content) of American coins should be the same as that of the British, so American and British coinage would be easy to exchange in international transactions. And he specified that foreign coins could continue to circulate legally in the United States for two or three years, until American coins could replace them.

At first, Hamilton provided for gold dollars and half-dollars in the coinage. However, because the high price of gold would necessitate small-size coinage, costly to misplace, Jefferson (the new secretary of state) and Congress rejected these coins. They settled on a system based on silver and gold—a bimetallic standard—at the ratio of 15:1. That is, a given amount of gold

This statue commemorates Alexander Hamilton, who called for the creation of a national mint.

would be worth 15 times the same amount of silver. The United States became the first nation to establish this standard.

The Mint Is Born

In 1792, Congress passed the Mint Act, establishing the United States Mint. The act specified Philadelphia as the location of the mint and provided for a director, assayer, chief coiner, engraver, treasurer, and workmen. It also specified the coin denominations to be minted and required that "an impression emblematic of Liberty" and the word "Liberty" had to appear on coins. It fixed the bimetallic rate at 15:1 (silver to gold) and allowed individuals to bring gold and silver to the mint to be coined for free.

Initially, the mint was placed under the jurisdiction of Jefferson's Department of State. In 1799, the mint became an independent department reporting directly to the president and authorized to make three types of coinage. Gold coins consisted of the eagle ($10), the half-eagle ($5), and the quarter-eagle ($2.50). Silver coins were quarter-dollars (25 cents), dismes (10 cents), and half-dismes. Copper coins were cents and half cents.

In this painting by John Ward Dunsmore, Martha Washington prepares to inspect one of the mint's first coins.

Washington rejected this sample bearing his likeness.

Copper patterns of the first designs proposed for the new currency depicted President Washington on the obverse and an eagle on the reverse. Congress did not approve the designs, however, and one representative, John Page, even warned that a bust of a living president seemed to flirt with the European or Roman pattern of honoring "Kings and Caesars." Page advised that such a portrait "would be viewed as a stamp of Royalty on our coins. . . ."

Washington agreed with Page and may have ordered the destruction of the dies, or stamps, from which those coins were made. Despite his desire not to have his portrait in every American's pocket, Washington took a keen interest in the coinage of the new nation. When the mint was established only a few hundred feet from his home in Philadelphia, Washington became a frequent visitor. And some of the first half-dismes it issued probably consisted of silver furnished by the president himself—perhaps George and Martha Washington's household silverware.

The first coins produced for circulation by the new mint in Philadelphia depicted a female head or figure of Liberty as a symbol of American independence. Although the female figure was only symbolic, artists sometimes used wives or girlfriends as models. Liberty often appeared wearing the round Phrygian cap worn by freed slaves in ancient Greece.

31

President Washington's appointee, scientist David Rittenhouse, directed construction of the first mint building.

THREE

Development of the Mint and Coinage

After the passage of the Mint Act of 1792, President Washington appointed David Rittenhouse, the foremost American scientist of the time, as head of the new mint. Rittenhouse, a self-educated clock maker, astronomer, and mathematician, had served as a member of Congress and as a professor of astronomy at the University of Pennsylvania.

Rittenhouse purchased the original site for the mint—three lots in Philadelphia. An abandoned, wood-framed whiskey distillery stood on one of the lots, but he quickly replaced it with a brick and stone structure, the first public building constructed by the United States government. The basement contained vaults holding silver and gold; the horse stables housed the copper stores. The first floor was divided into deposit and weighing rooms and a press room for gold coins. The second floor contained offices; the third held assay facilities for testing metals.

On the same site as the mint building stood a separate, horse-powered mill for the rolling machines and a smelter furnace. These buildings burned in 1816, and steam power replaced horsepower to drive the mint's metalworking equipment. But even with the new steam-powered machinery, the mint was more like a large blacksmith shop than like a modern factory. Furnaces and bellows created superhot fires for the melting of metals, and blacksmiths and metalworkers held many of the mint's most important jobs.

Because of the mint's precious metals and valuable equipment, all mint employees had to post bonds. In addition, workers could not leave the premises during work hours—not even for lunch. At night, a watchman patrolled the grounds, armed with a long dagger, pistol, and alarm bell—and aided by a watchdog. In fact, dog food was an official part of the mint budget.

Before steam power, horses drove mint machinery.

Early Coinage

Because Congress hadn't appropriated funds to buy bullion (bars of crudely prepared metal), the mint couldn't begin making coins until individuals brought nuggets, metallic dust, or bullion to be converted to coins for their own use. The early coining process demanded an understanding of the principles of metallurgy as well as craftsmanship, artistry, mechanical ability, and physical strength. The steps involved in the coining process clearly demonstrate the abilities of the nation's early coin makers.

As the first step, mint assayers tested the metal to determine its exact content. They scraped a small, precise amount of metal off the original nugget or bar, then wrapped the sample in a cone of lead sheets and placed it in a small bone-ash dish called a cupel. (Cupels were made from animal bones, kept behind the mint in an alley—appropriately called Bone Alley.) They then placed the lead-wrapped sample, in the cupel, in a 4,000° Fahrenheit (2,204° Centigrade) furnace.

As the assayer heated the sample, base—or nonprecious—metals (such as iron) oxidized, ran off with other oxides from the lead wrapping, and were eventually absorbed by the porous bone dish. The assayer could determine the precious metal content of the remaining sample with some precision by comparing its weight with the weight of a sample of known precious metal content that he had subjected to the same process. He could then separate silver from gold with nitric acid (which dissolves silver but not gold).

Refining, the second step in the process, was similar to assaying, but on a larger scale. Refiners separated base metals from silver and gold in a furnace, then made an alloy (a precise mixture of specific metals) as required by Congress for coins. In making the alloy for gold coins, they mixed gold—a relatively soft metal—with small, precise amounts of harder metals, such as silver or copper, so that gold coins would not wear out too silver or copper, so that gold coins would not wear out too quickly. Then they melted the refined metals, in correct alloy proportions, into brick-like blocks called ingots.

Rolling, the third step in coinage, flattened the ingots into strips of coin-size thickness. Horses drove a system of gears to operate the rollers. After a worker annealed (heated to soften) the ingots, he ran them through the rollers as many as ten times to achieve the desired thinness. Skilled craftsmen then drew or stretched these strips to the proper length in drawing machines.

In the fourth process, planchet-cutting, the planchet cutter (a large, threaded, steel cylinder with sharp edges) punched coin-size planchets—or blank coins—from the alloyed strips. The blanks then fell into a basket below the press. Milling took place in a separate machine, in which the operator placed the planchets between two toothed gears. He then gave a slight turn on a large, spoked wheel resembling the wheel of a ship. When the

After they separated gold and silver from base metals in huge furnaces, refiners cast brick-like ingots.

As horses powered the machinery from a pit below, workers flattened ingots by feeding them into rolling machines.

teeth of the gears moved across the planchet, they inscribed the milling marks.

The fifth and most delicate step was stamping the coins with dies (devices for reproducing patterned impressions, similar in effect to rubber stamps). To make a die, an engraver took a cylinder of steel with a highly polished face and covered the face with a special wax. He then took the drawing of the central coin design (for example, the Liberty head) and rubbed it off onto the wax. Very carefully, he cut the design into the steel, forming a "master die." This wasn't used to make coins, however, because it could crack and make production of identical coins practically impossible. Instead, the engraver used a hub (a mirror image of the master die) to make working dies that stamped the coins. If a working die broke—as often happened in the early mass production of coins—he could make an identical one from the master. Separate working dies stamped the central design and the outside lettering and dates.

Stamping machines—similar to planchet cutters—consisted of screw presses with the working die for one side of the coin attached to the cylinder, and the die for the other side on the base. The operator placed a planchet between the two dies, then heaved a long, weighted lever to turn the threaded cylinder, bringing it down to press the designs into the blank.

Early coin makers produced carefully crafted and relatively uniform coins with this five-step process. From 1793 until 1795, the mint produced 11,502 gold pieces, 614,351 silver pieces, and 1,832,720 coppers—despite the fact that making one suitable coin could take several minutes.

Cutting machines formed blank coins, called planchets, by stamping thin strips of metal with a steel-edged cutter.

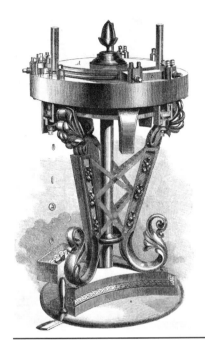

Milling machines put the ridges on the edges of planchets.

In 1833, the government completed a new, larger mint in Philadelphia, built in an imposing, classical style. The new mint provided considerably more room for operations than the earlier facilities had. It introduced steam coining presses there in 1836, and many other improvements over the years, particularly automatic feeding devices to handle the blanks and coins. In addition to increasing the speed of coin making, automatic feeding helped the workers, who were in jeopardy of losing a finger when "hand-feeding" the heavy machinery.

The discovery of gold lured thousands of fortune-seekers to the South and West and saved the mint from a metal shortage.

FOUR

The Mint Branches Out

On a Sunday morning in 1799, Conrad Reed, age 12, of Cabarras County, North Carolina, found an odd yellow rock while fishing. The Reed family used it as a doorstop for several years, but in 1802, Mr. Reed showed the 17-pound (7.65-kilogram) stone to a jeweler. It was nearly pure gold. The nation's first gold rush had begun.

Soon, miners discovered the "Southern Gold Region," stretching from Virginia to Alabama. These discoveries and others in the South and West would help save the national mint from a shortage of metals and would lead to the building of new mints in the country's developing regions.

At first, gold production in the South proceeded slowly. Poor transportation there made the Philadelphia mint and its coining services difficult to reach, but by 1820, enough southern gold reached Philadelphia to relieve a shortage that had kept the mint operating only part time. Federal coins were slow to make their way back to the gold regions, however, and soon local

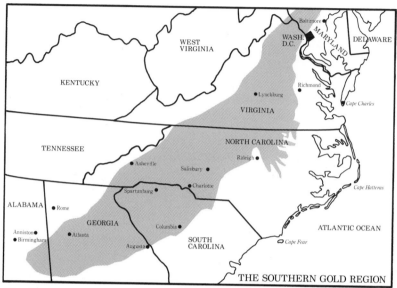

The Southern Gold Region (shaded above) ran from Virginia to Alabama. Discoveries here saved the mint from a metal shortage.

craftsmen, such as the Bavarian immigrant Christopher Bechtler, began to design and produce their own coins. (Thus, parts of the United States used privately minted coins as a medium of exchange even though they were not coined under the government's authority.)

In 1828, Americans elected Andrew Jackson as the nation's seventh president. This shrewd Tennessee landowner committed himself to expanding economic activity in the South and West. But these ambitions quickly brought him into conflict with the Philadelphia-based Second Bank of the United States, which had been founded in 1816 to succeed the First Bank of the United States when its charter expired.

The Second Bank was a government-chartered private bank that received government and private deposits. Located near the mint and run by wealthy Philadelphian Nicholas Biddle, the Second Bank controlled the exchange of its own national bank notes (paper money) for those issued by the state-chartered banks.

These national notes were especially useful in business transactions, because they were backed by (exchangeable for) the gold and silver deposits of the federal government. By coordinating loans and the exchange of notes across the country, the Second Bank had great economic power—the power of a "central bank."

President Jackson, along with many westerners and southerners, disapproved of Biddle's Philadelphia bank. Jackson's supporters, the Jacksonians, believed that Biddle's bank made most of its loans to eastern banks and denied loans to other areas of the nation. The Jacksonians did not want one national bank controlling the government's currency. They wanted to take this authority away from Biddle and his Second Bank and give it to the state banks.

The Jacksonians also believed that greater circulation of hard money (gold and silver deposits) would promote the growth of the nation's more remote regions. Everyone recognized and valued gold and silver coins—unlike state bank notes, which tended to be worth less the farther they traveled from the state where they were issued.

In 1832, Jackson refused to renew the charter of the Second Bank, thereby abolishing it as a federal agency. The following year, he withdrew public funds from the bank and sent them to state banks around the country. But even after the Second Bank's federal charter expired in 1836, Biddle continued to run it under a Pennsylvania state license.

New Mints in the South

To weaken the power of the Philadelphia bank and to increase the circulation of hard money, the Jacksonians convinced Congress to establish three new branch mints. One was in New Orleans, the port of entry for much of the foreign metal used in United States coinage. Two others were in the Southern Gold

Region—one in Charlotte, North Carolina, and one in Dahlonega, Georgia. The Jacksonians in Congress ensured that the branches were far from the Philadelphia mint—and far from Biddle's influence.

In establishing the mints, the government faced many problems. For example, no railways existed in the northern part of central Georgia until after the Civil War. Thus, all supplies for the Dahlonega mint, completed in 1837, had to be hauled up mountain roads by horse-drawn wagon. And the Charlotte mint building burned in 1844 and wasn't rebuilt until 1846.

Despite these problems, in the years before the Civil War, the Dahlonega and Charlotte mints manufactured about $12 million worth of gold coins for the federal government. The coins included half-eagles ($5), quarter-eagles ($2.50), gold dollars, and—in 1854 only—a $3 gold piece. The New Orleans mint, located at the port of entry for foreign metals, produced several times as many gold and silver coins as the other two branches.

Western Mints

Supplies of gold for the mints became plentiful when the California gold rush began in 1848. In 1850, California became part of the United States as a result of the war with Mexico in 1846 to 1848, and Congress authorized the opening of an assay office in San Francisco. (Assay offices tested the precious-metal content of samples but did not coin money.) In 1852, Congress opened a full-scale mint in San Francisco, which began producing gold and silver coins in 1854.

Miners also discovered gold in the West's mountain regions. They struck large amounts of gold in Colorado in 1859 and 1860. A private firm named Clark, Gruber & Company produced coins at its two-story "Mint & Bank" in Denver. These gold pieces bore the firm's name and a picture of Pike's Peak. The coins circulated throughout the West and were highly valued, because

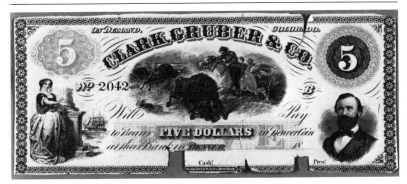

Clark, Gruber & Company produced coins and bank notes until the government bought the private firm in 1862.

they were made to nearly the same size and purity as federal coins. In 1862, the federal government purchased the Clark, Gruber & Company mint. Assaying operations began immediately, although the Denver mint did not actually begin producing federal coins until 1906.

The Civil War put an end to the manufacture of coins at Charlotte and Dahlonega. In 1861, after Georgia declared its secession from the Union, a Dahlonega businessman attempted to seize the mint and its gold. The mint's employees prevented the takeover, but they had to abandon the mint during the war. The Charlotte mint also ceased operations with the outbreak of hostilities, and southern troops were later housed there. After the war, the government put the Charlotte mint back into service as an assay office, but gold discoveries in the West and the re-opening of the New Orleans mint in 1879 convinced federal officials that coinage at the two smaller mints was unnecessary.

During the Civil War, the need for supplies and troops created a monetary crisis. The mint responded by developing new coins.

FIVE

The Civil War
and the Battle
of the Standards

The United States Civil War, which lasted from 1861 until 1865, began a 40-year conflict over America's monetary system. Before the war, the national government had collected the modest amounts of money needed for its activities through federal land sales and tariffs (taxes on goods imported into the nation from abroad). Federal income tax did not exist. Then, at the outbreak of the Civil War, the Union government suddenly needed extraordinary amounts of money—to buy guns, railroad cars, and supplies, and to feed and pay its soldiers. But President Jackson had abolished the Bank of the United States—the centralized national bank—in the 1830s. Now, in the 1860s, President Abraham Lincoln desperately needed to reassert centralized government control to finance the war and keep the economy running.

Early in the war, Lincoln's secretary of the treasury, Salmon P. Chase, persuaded some northern bankers to pay gold for Union war bonds. These new gold reserves enabled the Treas-

Secretary Chase built up gold reserves so the Union could print more paper money.

ury Department to print paper money to pay for government needs. But as the North's generals failed to win decisive battles against the South, investors lost confidence in the Union's paper money and exchanged it for specie, which they hoarded or sent abroad. The lack of specie caused a crisis. It forced the government to suspend specie payments—to stop issuing coin on demand in exchange for other forms of money.

Without an effective circulating coinage, the Union money system rapidly fell apart. "Greenbacks" (government paper money that could not be redeemed for specie) circulated at a discount—that is, they were worth less than their declared face value. People who needed money to make change started using foreign coins and postage stamps. The Treasury Department even began to issue American stamps without glue on the backs. The Treasury also put "shinplasters," bills in denominations of less than a dollar, into circulation.

Coins for War

During the Civil War, mint officials tried to help the government solve the Union's financial crisis. Even before the war, officials had suggested smaller, lighter coins and had proposed new alloys of silver, aluminum, and brass. The mint had also produced samples of annular, or ring-like, currency. These coins had holes in the centers that allowed them to be tied together or stacked on sticks for easy handling—an idea that was borrowed from the Chinese.

After more than two years of bloody and inconclusive fighting, Union Generals Ulysses S. Grant and William T. Sherman began to win victories for the North, which encouraged people to buy more Union bonds. These victories and the creation of a new National Banking System in 1863 made drastic changes in United States coinage unnecessary. The new banking system provided uniform national regulations for state banks, and the value of notes from banks that followed these rules was more secure. Still, the mint made some coinage changes that helped restore order to the chaotic Union money supply. These changes included the minting of a bronze penny and a new bronze 2-cent piece in 1864, and the authorization of a copper-nickel 3-cent piece in 1865. Secretary Chase also ordered the addition of the motto "In God We Trust" to all American coins, reflecting the Union's growing belief in victory. In 1866, less than a year after the war's end, the mint produced the nation's first nickel 5-cent piece.

The Confederates never developed a circulating coinage. Although a Philadelphia engraver designed and made a few sample coins for the South, southern mint personnel who were loyal to the Union wrecked the machinery and smashed the dies at the

Greenbacks became worth less than their face value.

Grant's victories inspired people to buy Union bonds and helped restore order to the money supply.

outbreak of the war. The Confederate states printed bales of paper money, but they lacked the organization, technology, and time needed to mass produce coins. This failing contributed to their defeat.

The Battle of the Standards

A financial controversy faced the mint at the end of the Civil War. The issue was silver and its place in the nation's monetary system. The bimetallic standard of 15:1 (silver to gold), established in 1792, had been raised to 16:1 in 1834. The bimetallic ratio meant that a specified amount of either of the two metals equaled one dollar, and individuals could present unlimited amounts of either metal for coinage. The gold discoveries of the 1840s and 1850s, however, made gold more available in the United States. In response to this, Congress lowered the ratio to 14.8:1. But at this ratio, the silver in a silver dollar increased in value abroad—to about $1.03. By simply stepping over the Canadian border, then, an investor could make $300 on $10,000 in American silver dollars. Soon, silver dollars disappeared from circulation in the United States as investors bought them up and took them out of the country.

After the Civil War, however, silver's value on the foreign market declined, removing the incentive for Americans to send silver abroad. In addition, miners were discovering large amounts of new silver in the West. In 1876, when the United States resumed the specie payments that had been suspended during the Civil War, American silver miners promptly appeared at the mints wanting all of their new silver coined into dollars. Much to their surprise, however, the mints would purchase only small amounts of silver, enough to make coins of less than a dollar.

This pro-silver political cartoon predicted that adoption of the gold standard would destroy prosperity.

Congress had passed the Coinage Act of 1873, which enabled the mints to do this.

Without the government purchases, silver surpluses started to pile up and silver prices began to fall. The miners were furious. So were small-scale farmers, who were concerned about the declining prices of agricultural goods and who hoped an influx of new silver dollars would help them pay off their loans and buy new seed and equipment. They charged that mint officials, influential Republican senators, and wealthy eastern bankers and bondholders had known of the coming silver surpluses and had prevented silver from coming back into circulation. The wealthy easterners, the farmers and miners charged, had made their fortunes in Civil War profits and didn't want "cheap" silver money in circulation or as payment for the small farmers' mounting debts. The gold advocates, or "gold bugs," on the other hand, argued that a "sound currency" limited to gold would encourage those with wealth to invest it in economic growth. Angered by that view, the silver advocates, or "silverites," dubbed the Coinage Act "the Crime of 1873."

Eventually, the silverites gained popularity and forced the mint to coin some of the miners' silver into "trade dollars." Congress had authorized these silver dollars in 1873 to help America trade with China, where merchants preferred large, heavy silver coins similar to those introduced by the British. Although not legal as government currency inside the United States, trade dollars were used as money throughout the West, especially among Chinese laborers who helped build America's railways.

Although the United States didn't stop trading with China, the mint stopped producing trade dollars in 1878, when Congress passed the Bland-Allison Act. This act authorized federal purchases of silver for the coinage of a domestic silver dollar, the Morgan dollar, named after its designer, George T. Morgan.

The government still purchased only limited amounts of silver, however, and miners and farmers continued their battle to

The mint coined silver trade dollars to help America trade with China and to appease angry silver miners.

reestablish silver fully as a coinage metal. Some politicians tried to resolve the problem scientifically by having the mint make coins of a new alloy that combined gold, silver, and copper in economically "correct" proportions based on the value of those metals. The mint made samples of these "goloid" coins, but as silver prices continued to drop, the idea became too complex to implement. The Sherman Silver Purchase Act of 1890 authorized more government purchases of silver, but Congress repealed the act in 1893 as a result of the efforts of President Grover Cleveland. A "Gold Democrat," Cleveland believed silver coinage was worsening the severe economic depression of the mid-1890s. The battle of the standards thus grew into a political and economic crisis.

The Populist Movement

The depression of the 1890s spurred the silverite cause. Hard-hit farmers had already formed Farmers Alliances—cooperatives to sell, store, and finance agricultural goods—enabling them to keep the profits that would have gone to the railroads, banks, and large grain storage companies. The alliances wanted reforms that would enable small farmers to retain control of their farms and to avoid becoming factory workers or laborers on others' farms. Also among their demands was the "free and unlimited coinage of silver at the ratio of 16 to 1." These mostly western and southern agricultural groups soon helped to form a third political party, the People's Party, or Populists.

The Populists elected many of their candidates in the 1892 and 1894 congressional elections and seemed to be on the verge of becoming a party equal to the Democrats and Republicans. Meanwhile, President Cleveland, the "Gold Democrat," had lost control of his party, and the popular William Jennings Bryan, a Nebraskan who favored silver, became the Democratic front-runner. Some Populists wanted to unite with the Democrats for the 1896 presidential election. Others feared that the Populists' farm reforms would be lost if the two parties united on the silver issue. But Bryan captured the new party's support with dramatic flair. Throwing his arms out wide, he ended his convention speech with a cry of accusation against the Republicans: "You shall not crucify mankind on a cross of gold!" Bryan was nominated.

Bryan won his party's nomination with an emotional speech against the gold standard.

This preelection cartoon lampooned Bryan and the silver standard. The caption read, "Take your choice of the two bills!"

The presidential election pitted Democrat-Populist Bryan against Republican William McKinley, who opposed unlimited silver coinage. Although a few "Silver Republicans" from the mining states supported Bryan, McKinley won the election with the help of urban voters, businessmen, bankers, and the Cleveland Gold Democrats. The election destroyed the Farmers Alliances and the Populist party, as well as the silverites' chance to restore the full bimetallic standard. And the discovery of huge amounts of new gold in Alaska and South Africa put more gold coin into circulation. In 1900, Congress passed the Gold Standard Act, officially ending bimetallism and putting the nation on the gold standard. The mint would still coin some silver dollars, but the battle of the standards was over.

From 1896 to 1918, the mint mass-produced coins for many foreign countries as well as the United States.

SIX

The United States as a World Money Power

The establishment of gold as the national standard opened a new era in American politics and economics. Gold-backed currency enabled American investors and traders to compete effectively with the gold-standard European nations for a larger share of world trade and investment. The design of a new banking system, the construction of new mint facilities, and the production of new coins helped American leaders shape institutions that would expand the nation's power abroad.

Like the European nations, the United States acquired overseas territories at the turn of the century. As a result of its victory in the Spanish-American War of 1898, the United States took control of Cuba, Puerto Rico, and the Philippines. But in the new international economic competition of the time, many American leaders were less interested in possessing colonies than in maintaining an "open door" abroad for profitable American trade and investment. Lyman J. Gage—a Chicago banker, a gold

The Spanish-American War opened trade with Latin America.

standard supporter, and President McKinley's secretary of the treasury—remarked that in international economic competition, a gold standard "war chest" was as important as "war ships . . . or regiments of men."

The United States had taken a tentative first step into international currency when the mint manufactured coins for Venezuela in 1875. But between 1896 and the end of World War I, in 1918, the American mint began to mass-produce coins for Colombia, Costa Rico, Cuba, the Dominican Republic, Ecuador, El Salvador, Mexico, Nicaragua, Panama, Peru, and the Philippines. As part of the United States' efforts to expand its influence in the world economic system, Presidents Theodore Roosevelt, William Howard Taft, and Woodrow Wilson also sent American financial experts to the less developed countries of Latin America and Asia. Experts such as Charles A. Conant worked to make the currencies of these nations more compatible with the gold-standard system used by the United States and other countries. By 1905, for example, the "conant," a coin worth exactly 50 cents in United States money, had become part of the Philippine money system.

The Mint and the Federal Reserve

Although the 1863 National Banking Act had created a loose association of national banks, the United States had been without a central bank since Andrew Jackson's time. The severe depression of the 1890s convinced many financial and corporate leaders that the United States again needed central banking. They remembered how, to save their reserves from depletion during an 1890s money panic, the national banks and the government had had to appeal to international financier J.P. Morgan to loan gold to the government. This had embarrassed the national bankers and the government and placed immense power in Morgan's hands.

So after America's entry into the contest for world markets, American bankers and Treasury officials began to study European central banking methods and to discuss a new central bank for the United States. Their goal was to use a central bank's power to mobilize American finances for world economic competition and to prevent or make less severe the kinds of economic crises they had experienced during the 1890s. Central bank advocates included Treasury Secretary Gage and Mint Director George E. Roberts. But many state and local bankers still feared the power of large eastern banks, and they pressured Congress not to create a central bank.

In 1902, Secretary Gage retired, and President Roosevelt appointed Leslie M. Shaw as secretary of the treasury. Shaw also favored increasing government's control over the national money supply as a way of counteracting financial crises. But knowing that many in Congress opposed the creation of a new central bank, Shaw used his power as treasury secretary to do what a central bank might do—loan government cash reserves to national banks when he felt it would help the economy.

Shaw's actions directly affected the national mint and its branches, which were official subtreasuries—depositories for the government's cash reserves. According to the law that established the subtreasuries, the treasury secretary could give the mint director and the treasurers of each mint authority over the mint's reserves. If Shaw's experiments in shifting government

*Secretary Shaw pushed for
increased government control of
the nation's money supply.*

money became policy, as he hoped, the mint would become part
of a powerful "central bank" run from within the Treasury Department. But many in Congress, even those who favored central banking, believed that official approval of Shaw's actions
would give the treasury secretary too much power—the power
of a potential economic czar. They rejected Shaw's plans.

Shaw's efforts to use the mint and subtreasuries as part of
a Treasury Department central bank helped political and corporate leaders unite to create an independent Federal Reserve System. Established by Congress in 1913, the Federal Reserve System functioned as a central bank—America's first since the
1830s. The architects of the Federal Reserve System, mindful of
the traditional hostility to eastern bankers, enlisted the support
of bankers from every region and placed branches in twelve cities
across the nation. In 1920, the Federal Reserve System elim-
inated the subtreasuries, so the mint never became a great financial power on its own. But it continued to store United States
bullion reserves and now distributes the nation's coinage through
the Federal Reserve Banks.

New Mint Facilities

By the early 1900s, the demand for domestic and foreign coins
exceeded the mint's ability to supply them. A growing population

and the end of the 1890s depression contributed to the shortage, as did the advent of vending machines, which required large supplies of well-made, uniform coins.

To supply the country with needed coinage, the government opened a massive new mint in Philadelphia, in 1901. The lobby, finished in Italian marble, with gold-backed, glass-tile ceilings, featured mosaics illustrating ancient coin making. Louis C. Tiffany, the renowned stained-glass artist, supervised the mosaic work. (These mosaics were remounted in the present United States Mint, built in the late 1960s on Independence Mall in Philadelphia.)

Twentieth-Century Coins

In 1906, President Theodore Roosevelt decided to make new designs for American coins his own special project. He commissioned the famous sculptor Augustus St. Gaudens to redesign U.S. gold pieces in a classical high-relief style. The early St. Gaudens designs used Roman numerals for dates. The reverse featured the American eagle in flight over a sun with rays (a Roman imperial symbol); the obverse showed Liberty striding forth with torch and olive branch (a symbol of peace). The obverse of another St. Gaudens coin depicted Liberty in an Indian eagle-feather headdress. Roosevelt hoped that illustrations that

This St. Gaudens gold piece featured Liberty in an Indian headdress on the obverse and the American eagle on the reverse.

resembled those of ancient Rome and Greece would emphasize America's position as one of the great empires of history. But when Roosevelt excluded the motto "In God We Trust" from the St. Gaudens coins, many citizens and legislators objected. Congress, with Roosevelt's agreement, reinstated the words on the coins in 1908.

The tradition, established by Washington, of not using famous leaders on coinage ended in 1909—the centennial of Lincoln's birth. President Roosevelt commissioned the engraver Victor D. Brenner to prepare a commemorative medallion honoring the occasion. The incoming Taft administration released the Brenner portrait of Lincoln on a new 1-cent coin—the Lincoln portrait still appears on the penny. The Great Emancipator's contribution to freedom was unquestionable, and the public greeted his portrait with enthusiasm.

Other coins depicting famous historical figures followed the Lincoln penny. In 1932, the 200th anniversary of George Washington's birth, the mint issued the first Washington quarter, which replaced the Standing Liberty quarter. The current Thomas Jefferson nickel appeared in 1938, replacing the Buffalo/Indian Head nickel of 1913. About a year after Franklin Delano Roosevelt's death, the mint introduced the Roosevelt dime in 1946, commemorating Roosevelt's support for the March of Dimes against polio, of which he was a victim. The mint issued the John F. Kennedy half-dollar in 1964, the year after his assassination. And in 1979, it produced the Susan B. Anthony dollar, honoring the American suffragist.

Silver-mining interests played a role in early 20th-century minting. In 1918, the Pittman Act authorized the mint to melt down 350 million silver dollars to sell to manufacturers who needed silver during World War I. After the war, the government ordered the mint to buy back an equal amount of silver and coin it into dollars or keep it as a reserve. One result was the 1921 Peace Dollar, featuring a portrait of Liberty.

When the World War I silver shortage ended, the mint bought back tons of silver and minted the 1921 Peace Dollar.

Off the Gold Standard

During the Great Depression of the 1930s, the Federal Reserve attempted to relieve the economic crisis by making gold reserves available. Businesses feared further price declines, however, and they bought and hoarded gold. To prevent shortages in the nation's gold reserves, President Roosevelt—employing the executive powers of the Trading with the Enemy Act of 1917—revised practices that allowed the exchange of paper currency for gold. Congress quickly backed the president by passing the Emergency Banking Act in 1933.

In 1934, Congress made another attempt to stimulate the nation's economy by passing the Gold Reserve Act, reducing the gold content of the dollar from 23.22 grains (the content since 1837) to 13.71 grains. This change allowed the government to issue more paper dollars. The nation's gold reserves continued to stand for United States currency, but with the nation off the gold standard, this currency was no longer exchangeable for gold. As a result, the mint refused gold for coinage, and Americans were forbidden to hoard gold bullion. These restrictions continued even after World War II, when the United States became the world's leading power.

Artists such as chief sculptor-engraver Elizabeth Jones design the nation's coins.

SEVEN

Today's Mint— People and Powers

Today's United States Mint, a bureau of the Department of the Treasury, occupies a position similar to that of other Treasury subdivisions, such as the Bureau of Engraving and Printing, the U.S. Customs Service, and the Internal Revenue Service. In fact, the mint and the Bureau of Engraving and Printing (the maker of the nation's paper currency and other specially prepared documents) are two of the largest government manufacturing operations.

Who's in Charge

The director of the mint reports to the secretary of the treasury through the treasurer of the United States. Appointed by the president, with the advice and consent of the Senate, the director serves a renewable five-year term. Other presidential appointments include the positions of superintendents of the Philadelphia and Denver mints and of the West Point Bullion

The United States Mint Organization

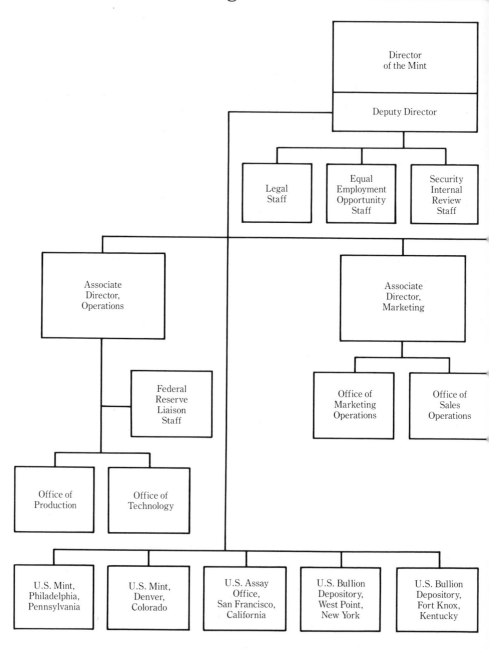

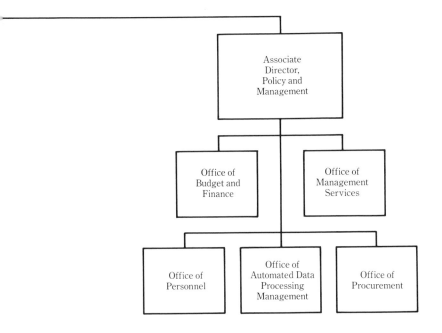

Depository and such traditional positions as the chief sculptor-engraver and the assayer.

The mint's headquarters, in Washington D.C., acts as the center of mint administration and of coinage research and development. Mint activities here fall into four major divisions, one headed by the deputy director of the mint, who works with the director, and the other three headed by associate directors. The director and deputy director supervise the mint's legal staff, equal opportunity program, and security. In addition, they oversee the five major production and storage branches of the mint—in Philadelphia, Denver, San Francisco, West Point, and Fort Knox, Kentucky. The associate directors supervise the mint's operations, marketing, and policy and management activities.

The Civil Service Commission supplies most of the mint's approximately 2,000 employees. Students add to that number by serving summer internships. Because the mint functions primarily as a manufacturing operation, the majority of mint employees are hands-on production workers, men and women who operate and repair the machines, design the mint's products, and check the quality of the coins. The rest of the employees work in

The Philadelphia Mint Building is one of five production and storage centers located throughout the country.

Most mint employees do production work, such as counting and bagging coins.

nonproduction areas, such as statistical analysis, research and development, procurement of supplies and services, management, and security.

Currently, the mint purchases many of its goods and services from, and assigns many of its research projects to, private corporations. Corporations also provide the supplies needed for numismatic (coin collecting) items, such as coin bags, display cases, refined coinage metals, 1-cent coin blanks, cupronickel strips used for nickels, and copper-and-nickel bonded (or clad) coinage strips used for dimes, quarters, and half-dollars. In addition, the mint employs private distributors to expand sales of— and increase its income from—numismatic items.

Congress and the Mint

The mint, subject to congressional coinage laws, reports regularly to Congress. The mint's director, accompanied by legal and administrative assistants, appears regularly at hearings held by

A congressional subcommittee reviews the mint's budget and activities. Congress also decides which coins will be minted.

the Subcommittee on Coinage and Consumer Affairs of the House Committee on Banking, Finance, and Urban Affairs. This committee's responsibilities include listening to public opinion on the mint, guiding the mint's appropriation requests through Congress, and reviewing mint activities and policies. The committee may also legislate changes in mint policies and activities—as long as Congress passes the legislation.

Legislation also determines what coins are manufactured. The mint can only produce denominations—including commemorative coins—authorized by law. Also, the designs of circulating U.S. coins cannot change more frequently than every 25 years without special legislation. At that time, the mint director may propose and implement new designs, with the approval of the secretary of the treasury and after consultation with the Commission of Fine Arts (appointed by the president) on the artistic merit of the designs.

Congress may pass laws demanding changes in coin design and composition; it may also direct the mint to prepare samples of new coin designs and types. For example, during World War II, Congress authorized the mint to produce gray pennies of zinc-coated steel, which helped conserve copper for military usage. In 1982, when a rise in the market price of copper caused the mint's production cost for pennies to approach the pennies' face value, Congress authorized the shift to the current copper-plated zinc penny, saving the government millions of dollars.

To handle production costs, the mint requests and receives about $48 million a year from Congress. However, it returns unspent funds—sometimes amounting to as much as $7 million—to the government's general fund. In addition, coin collectors provide it with annual revenues of up to $300 million on numismatic sales. And the mint adds more than $500 million to the government's coffers in seignorage, the difference between the cost of manufacturing a coin and the face value of the coin. For example, a penny might cost only .6 cent to manufacture, adding .4 cent to government funds. Coin seignorage, like the printing of paper money, adds an artificial wealth to the money system, offset to some extent by the destruction of mutilated coinage. The mint reports figures on seignorage, so that Congress and the Treasury Department can determine its effect on the economy.

The sale of rare coins and other numismatic items adds more than $300 million to the mint's coffers annually.

Mint Responsibilities

According to a law introduced in 1973, the director of the mint may authorize any mint facility to produce needed coinage. For example, mint directors have authorized the San Francisco and West Point facilities to produce extra domestic coins. They purposely make sure that these limited-production coins contain no mint marks (the tiny initials that usually identify the source of production, such as "S" for San Francisco), because collectors save coins with unusual mint marks instead of spending them, which takes them out of circulation.

Usually, however, production of circulating coins takes place at the Philadelphia and Denver mints. (The Philadelphia mint supplies the engraving for all coins and medals.) Various branches produce, distribute, and sell the mint's collectors' items such as uncirculated coin sets. Mint marks are purposely included on these items to stimulate demand among collectors for coin varieties. The Mint Museum, housed at the San Francisco Old Mint and run by the Assay Office, exhibits historic coins and coining equipment.

The mint maintains and guards gold reserves at the United States Bullion Depositories at Fort Knox, Kentucky, and at West Point, New York. The Fort Knox building, constructed in 1936, stores only gold. Fences and sentry boxes surround the building, which is made of granite, steel, and concrete. Fort Knox allows no visitors and provides tight—extremely tight—security. The depository houses gold in brick-size bars, each weighing about 27.5 avoirdupois pounds (12.5 kilograms). The gold content of each bar is 400 troy ounces (12,441.2 grams), a special weight measurement used for precious metals. By the mid-1980s, the gold in each bar was worth more than $130,000. The West Point Depository, originally completed in 1938 to house silver, now houses both gold and silver bullion, as does the Denver mint. The San Francisco Assay Office stores silver bullion. The United

States Mint supplies its own security at the various depositories but receives additional assistance from the army at Fort Knox.

Although the mint maintains its various buildings and facilities, the General Services Administration provides major construction, repairs, and renovations. Each of the five mint facilities has its own superintendent (a presidential appointee) or officer-in-charge (a career employee) and administrative staff, who oversee the facility's day-to-day operations. The head of each facility may hire permanent and temporary workers, but officials in Washington must authorize and budget all decisions.

The mint supplies circulation coins directly to the Federal Reserve System for distribution. The reserve, responsible for the release of coins to commercial banks, keeps the mint informed of its needs and also sorts through the circulating coinage, picking out foreign or counterfeit coins and returning bent or worn coins to the mint for melting and recoinage.

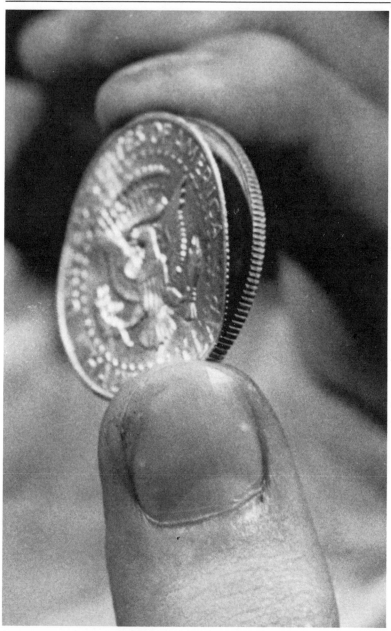

Thin layers of copper-nickel alloy are bonded to copper cores to make clad coins, which replaced solid coins in 1965.

EIGHT

Today's Mint at Work

America relies on the United States Mint to supply the nation's circulating coins. Although modernization has changed the manufacturing and production processes, the mint still provides the same basic services necessary for maintaining a federal coinage as it did in 1792.

Until the Coinage Act of 1965, the mint made dimes, quarters, and half-dollars from an alloy of 90 percent silver and 10 percent copper. Today, the mint produces these coins from strips of metal bonded together, a process called cladding. Copper lies in the center, visible as a stripe on the edges of coins. The outside strips are an alloy of 75 percent copper and 25 percent nickel. The Eisenhower dollar, made from 1971 to 1978, was a clad coin of this type—and the first dollar coin since 1935. The Susan B. Anthony dollar, minted in 1979 and 1980, was another clad coin, slightly larger than a quarter. Unfortunately, the Anthony dollar has not generated great demand, perhaps because some people fear confusing it with the quarter.

In the Susan B. Anthony dollar, copper is sandwiched between a copper-nickel alloy.

Nickels and pennies, unlike the higher-denomination coins, are not clad coins. Nickels are composed entirely of an alloy of 75 percent copper and 25 percent nickel. And, since 1983, all pennies have been made of copper-plated zinc, not the previous alloy of 95 percent copper and 5 percent zinc. Although the new pennies are the same size as the old copper cents, they weigh about 20 percent less.

The mint tests coins to assure that their metal content meets government standards. Citizens can send certain amounts of metal to the Philadelphia mint for testing and recoinage (for example, they can send pennies melted together in a house fire). In addition, individuals who think they have a counterfeit coin may send it to the mint for examination—although the mint cannot honor or return counterfeit coins.

Today's coinage process resembles that used in the mint's early days. The process is aided, however, by increasingly advanced materials and techniques. The old Philadelphia blacksmith shop is now a modern factory, with a more uniform product, more automatic procedures, and much larger yield. Between 1793 and 1795, the mint produced about 2 million coins, but in the peak year of 1982, it manufactured about 20 billion coins.

Public demand for coins—and consequently coin production—has dropped lately. (About 15 billion coins were made in 1985.) Whereas it once took the mint several minutes to make a single penny, today's Philadelphia mint is capable of producing nearly 45 million pennies in a three-shift, 24-hour workday.

Modern Manufacturing

In the current manufacturing process, each stroke of a hydraulic press punches dozens of blanks (or planchets) from wide strips of metal. A modern press runs at about 200 strokes a minute and sends showers of sparkling blanks into bins below it. The blanks are shaken on a mesh that allows undersize coins and "clips" (half-moon blanks from the edge of the strip) to fall through—a process called riddling. A chemical cleaning/polishing solution of argols, or cream of tartar, similar to that used during the 19th century, then cleans the blanks. But today, mechanized rotating

Large coin presses and advanced processing methods allow the mint to produce millions of coins per day, if necessary.

barrels that look like huge washers and dryers wash and dry the blanks.

In upsetting, the next step, a gas furnace heats the blanks. Machines roll—or "upset"—the coins' edges to raise a smooth rim. Dies then strike the coins one, two, or four at a time, and those requiring milled or reeded edges have the milling cut in as they are struck. Dies hit a penny with about 40 tons of force, a nickel with about 80 tons, and a 50-cent piece with about 100 tons. Larger coins and medals may take as much as 180 tons of force. The ability of modern-day steel die alloys to withstand these repeated smashing pressures allows today's quality and speed of manufacture. Today's working dies have a "die life" of about 800,000 to 1 million strikes.

The making of these coinage dies, still the most delicate and artistic aspect of production, differs greatly from the method of the early mint. Today, the mint's sculptor-engravers prepare a

Thousands of coins flow from the hydraulic presses.

A sculptor-engraver compares the Kennedy half-dollar's cast to a reduction.

model of the coin from a sketch designed in accordance with the law authorizing the coinage. They make the model in plastilene (a waxy, oil-based clay), usually 3 to 12 times larger than the actual coin. Then artists cast a plaster-of-paris negative from this model, cut the lettering, dates, and other details into it, and make a plaster positive for final approval.

After design approval, the engravers make a rubber negative and then an epoxy, hard-plastic positive. This epoxy positive fits on a Janvier transfer machine, a special machine that both copies the design and reduces it to coin size while engraving a tool-steel blank, called a hub. The process takes from 8 to 12 hours just for the first cut. A sensing rod runs over the surface of the model, as gears reduce the size and transmit the tiniest design details to the face of the hub. Machine oil dribbles across the hub face to lubricate the engraving tip and wash off metal fragments. After the engravers put the final touches on the hub by hand, it's hardened and used to produce the working dies used in the coining presses. The French introduced these "high-tech" machines nearly a century ago—a 90-year-old Janvier machine still cranks away at the Philadelphia mint.

Coin Production and Distribution

Regulating coin production and distribution presents a challenge equal to that of coin manufacturing. Recently, the United States Mint hired a private research corporation to provide short- and long-term forecasts to help it determine the number of coins to make. The mint generally attempts to overproduce coins, because it can release coins from inventory in response to a need more easily than it can produce them to meet a sudden shortage.

When calculating coin production, the mint also responds to the projections of the Federal Reserve System, which keeps its own statistics. Certain demand patterns, such as the increased need for coins around the Christmas season, have become well-known. Less easily predicted, but quite noticeable, are the effects of changes in retail sales policies. Mint officials also observe an altered demand for different coins when pay telephone rates go up or mass transit systems hike their fares.

The mint distributes coins through the Federal Reserve System, shipping pennies and nickels in large tractor-trailer trucks to the various Federal Reserve Banks while sending other coins by smaller armored carriers. Sometimes, the Philadelphia mint trucks its coins just across Independence Mall to the Federal Reserve branch there. Guards, armed with shotguns and radios, control traffic and supervise the process.

Special Mint Products

The mint makes available to collectors sets of newly minted coins called uncirculated coin sets. These limited-edition sets command higher-than-face-value prices. The mint also manufactures more expensive proof coin sets, produced only at the San Francisco Assay Office. Proof coins are regular designs made with great attention to detail. The dies and blanks undergo polishing and striking processes that give proof coins a mirrorlike finish.

The mint manufactures uncirculated coin sets, proof coins, and other products for collectors.

The United States Mint made commemorative coins, still usable as legal tender, for private sponsors from 1892 to 1954. The first commemorative was a special 50-cent piece in honor of the Columbian Exposition. Commemorative issues required the approval of the president, the House, and the Senate. After the mint produced the coins, it turned them over to their sponsors at face value. The sponsor then sold them at higher prices to raise money for a particular project or program. Commemoratives, minted in silver and gold, included coins honoring Lewis and Clark's expedition to the Northwest, centennials and other anniversaries, and historic figures, such as Booker T. Washington and George Washington Carver. Presidents Hoover, Franklin Roosevelt, Truman, and Eisenhower were reluctant to authorize too many commemorative issues, however. They feared that the coins might enter circulation and confuse the public, make counterfeiting easier, or create huge profits for coin dealers who might buy up the limited production.

Recently, the United States government has sponsored commemorative issues, including George Washington coins in 1982, Olympic coins from 1983 to 1984, and Statue of Liberty coins in 1986. Through an act of Congress, the money raised from the sale of these issues funds special concerns, such as the national debt, the Los Angeles Olympic Games, and the restoration of the Statue of Liberty and the Ellis Island immigration facilities. Some of these coins, like the mint's proof sets, are made from specially polished dies and blanks. The mint produces commemoratives in uncirculated versions as well. When official production ends, the mint has a ceremony and melts unsold coins and dies so production of additional coins cannot decrease the value of the original coinage.

In 1974, Congress lifted the depression-era prohibition on the private ownership of gold coins and gold bullion. In 1986, Congress authorized the mint to produce a new series of gold bullion coins in four denominations: 1-ounce, $50 coins; .5-ounce, $25 coins; .25-ounce, $10 coins; and .1-ounce, $5 coins. These 22-karat gold coins consist of about 92 percent gold, 3 percent silver, and 5 percent copper and sell at prices that vary with the market value of their precious metal—now much higher than the coins' face value. The $50 gold coin depicts Liberty on the ob-

The mint raises money for special causes by releasing commemorative coins, such as this 1984 gold piece.

Mint medals commemorate important events and people.

verse and a family of eagles on the reverse. Designed for investment and collection rather than circulation, the U.S. bullion coins compete internationally with the Canadian Maple Leaf gold coins and the South African Krugerrands (whose importation into the United States has been banned since September 1985 by Executive Order).

The mint is also producing a 1-ounce, silver bullion coin with a face value of $1. The silver coin depicts Liberty on the obverse and an eagle on the reverse.

As a secondary function, the mint produces and sells medals, which originated in colonial times as ceremonial gifts from settlers to Native Americans to commemorate treaties. One series of modern medals commemorates the achievements of Americans and foreigners—from poets and pilots to politicians and prizefighters. Another series duplicates in bronze the gold medals awarded to distinguished citizens. (The mint used to make military decorations, but recently discontinued their production.) Mint medals also celebrate centennials and bicentennials of important events and portray presidents, secretaries of the treasury, military heros, and mint directors. The mint also makes low-priced, miniature, bronze presidential medals especially for sale to young collectors.

Some time in the future, the mint may use robots to stack bags of freshly minted coins for storage.

NINE

New Challenges

Since 1792, the mint's mission has remained the same—to produce the circulating coinage of the United States. In its long history, the mint has evolved from a small Philadelphia workshop to one of the government's largest manufacturing organizations. Along the way, great names in American history have played a vital role in the mint's development: Thomas Jefferson, Alexander Hamilton, Andrew Jackson, and Theodore Roosevelt. Through depressions and times of prosperity, trade wars and political turmoil, struggles between small farmers and big business, and the needs of a nation at war and at peace, the mint has adapted. It has developed new methods of production, changed metallic standards, and removed certain coins from circulation while introducing others.

Today, the United States Mint faces a future of challenges. Modern technology and administration have helped the mint meet the challenge of production and will continue to do so. An experimental robot, for example, stacks bags of newly minted coins at the Philadelphia mint, and mint officials are studying the use of laser engraving. Increased use of automatic cash transfers, magnetic-strip cards for mass transport systems, and other technological innovations may decrease the need for coins.

The mint's policy of contracting private corporations to supply goods and services poses another challenge. For example, the mint has closed down its own gold refinery in New York as well as the Philadelphia strip mill, a metal factory that once took up half of the mint building. Administrators feel that outside contracting is more economical for the mint's limited production—especially given congressional budget cuts. But some members of Congress argue that the mint may become too dependent on its private suppliers. They believe it is the government's responsibility to make coins.

At one time, American coinage issues determined the fate of nations, presidents, and political parties. Today, the modern world takes coins for granted: a jingle in a pocket, pennies stored in a jar, or change for the soda machine.

Mint workers who belong to the American Federation of Government Employees feel the mint should rely on its employees instead of outside contractors.

And yet, coins help preserve the ideals of a nation "conceived in Liberty." The recent Statue of Liberty coin reflects the promise of freedom embodied in a symbol first required by the Mint Act of 1792: "an impression emblematic of Liberty." And coins continue to reflect the ways in which Americans work toward those ideals—the recent Susan B. Anthony dollar honors a woman who fought for the right to vote, at a time when women still fight for full equality. America's history and coinage remain permanently entwined.

GLOSSARY

Alloy – A precise mixture of specific metals.

Assay – To determine precious metal content.

Bimetallic standard – A monetary standard system based on a set ratio of silver to gold.

Bullion – Bars of crudely prepared metal.

Cladding – Bonding strips of metal together.

Die – Device for exactly reproducing patterned impressions, much like a rubber stamp.

Gold standard – The system used from 1900 to 1934 that tied the value of United States currency to gold.

Milling – Fine parallel lines stamped on the edges of precious-metal coins; also called reeding.

Numismatics – The study or collection of currency.

Obverse – The "heads" side of a coin.

Planchet – A blank coin.

Reverse – The "tails" side of a coin.

Seignorage – The difference between the cost of making a coin and its face value.

Specie – Metal of any kind in coin form.

Troy ounce – A weight used for precious metals that is slightly heavier than a standard ounce.

SELECTED REFERENCES

Bowers, Q. David. *Adventures With Rare Coins*. Los Angeles: Bowers & Ruddy Galleries, Inc., 1979.

Evans, George G. *History of the United States Mint and Coinage*. Long Island City, N.Y.: Sanford J. Durst, 1982.

Failor, Kenneth M., and Hayden, Eleonora. *Medals of the United States Mint*. Washington, D.C.: Government Printing Office, 1972.

Schwarz, Ted. *A History of United States Coinage*. San Diego: A.S. Barnes, 1980.

Stewart, Frank H. *History of the First United States Mint*. Lawrence, Mass.: Quarterman, 1974.

Taxay, Don. *The U.S. Mint and Coinage*. Long Island City, N.Y.: Sanford J. Durst, 1983.

ACKNOWLEDGMENTS

The author and publisher are grateful to these individuals and organizations for information and photographs: Augustine A. Albino, Head of the Office of Administration, Philadelphia Mint; American Federation of Government Employees; American Numismatic Society; Arco Publishing Co.; Chase Manhattan Bank Archive; Coin World; Colorado Historical Society; House of Representatives; Independence National Historical Park Collection; Library of Congress; Larry Stevens Coinpics; Jim Livingston; Eleanor McKelvey, Public Information Officer, Philadelphia Mint; Museum of the American Indian, Heye Foundation; Museum of Fine Arts, Boston; National Archives; National Portrait Gallery; New York Public Library Picture Collection; Smithsonian Institution; United States Mint; University of Maryland Photo Section; UPI/ Bettmann Newsphotos; Judith L. Wagner, Assistant Director of Management Services of United States Mint, Washington, D.C.; Washington Post, reprinted by permission of the D.C. Public Library; Wide World; Picture research: Domenico G. Firmani Associates, Inc.

INDEX

A

alloys 35–36, 48, 53, 75–76, 88
American Revolution 24–27
annealing 36
annular currency 48–49
Articles of Confederation 24, 26
assaying process 35, 88

B

bank notes 42–43
barter 21
Bechtler, Christopher 42
Biddle, Nicholas 42–43
bimetallic standard 29–30, 50–55, 88
Bland-Allison Act 52
bonds 48–49
branch mints 43–45
brass 24
Brenner, Victor D. 62
Brigden, Edward 25
bronze 49, 83
Bryan, William Jennings 54–55
budget 71
bullion 35, 63, 82–83, 88
Bureau of Engraving and Printing 18, 65
business 11, 13, 14, 19, 43, 59

C

California gold rush 44
central bank 29, 42–43, 58–60
Charlotte mint 44–45
Chase, Salmon P. 47, 49
China 52
Civil War 9, 19, 44–51
cladding 75, 88
Clark, Gruber & Company 44–45
Cleveland, Grover 53–55
clipping 23–24

Coinage Act of 1873 52
Coinage Act of 1905 75
coin production 33–39, 76–79
    regulation of 72, 80
    volume of 38, 76–77, 80
colonies 17, 21–26
Colorado 44–45
commemorative coins 81–82
Commission of Fine Arts 70
composition (of coins) 22–24, 26, 29, 30, 35, 44, 50–55, 70–71, 75–76, 82
Conant, Charles A. 58
conant 58
Constitution 17, 24, 28
Continental Congress 24, 26–27
Continental Congress Currency Committee 27
copper 27, 30–31, 35, 71, 75–76
counterfeiting 23–24, 29, 73, 76
cupel 35

D

Dahlonega mint 44–45
denominations (of coins) 26–27, 29, 30, 49, 62, 70, 75, 82
Denver mint 44–45, 71
Department of State 8, 18, 30
Department of the Treasury 8, 18, 47–48, 59–60, 65
Depression, Great 11, 63
depression of the 1890s 53, 59
design (of coins) 24–28, 30–31, 61–62, 70, 79, 82–83
dies 31, 37–38, 78–79, 88
director of the mint 65, 69–70, 72
distribution, coin 72–73, 80
doubloons, Spanish 22–23

E

Emergency Banking Act of 1933 63

employees, mint 65–68, 86

engraving 37–38, 78–79

F

Farmers Alliances 53–55

federal bank (see central bank)

Federal Reserve System 60, 63, 73, 80

Fort Knox 72, 73

Franklin, Benjamin 17, 25

G

Gage, Lyman J. 57–59

General Services Administration 73

Georgia 44–45

gold 22–24, 29, 30, 35, 41, 44, 47, 51–55, 57, 63, 72, 82–83

Gold Democrats 53–55

Gold Reserve Act of 1934 63

gold standard 55–58, 63, 88

Gold Standard Act 55

Great Britain 17, 22–23, 25, 29

greenbacks 48

guineas, French 22

H

Hamilton, Alexander 8, 11, 17, 28–30

Hamilton plan 26, 28–30

headquarters, mint 68

I

Indians (see Native Americans)

ingots 36

international trade 57–59

J

Jackson, Andrew 8, 9, 42–43

Jacksonians 43–44

Janvier transfer machine 79

Jefferson, Thomas 8, 11, 17, 18, 27, 62

Jefferson plan 26–27

johannes, Portuguese 22

K

Krugerrands, South African 83

L

legislation 69–71

Liberty 30–31, 61, 82, 87

limited-production coins 72, 80–83

Lincoln, Abraham 47, 62

M

Maple Leaf coins, Canadian 83

Massachusetts Bay Colony 22

McKinley, William 55

medals 83

metallurgy 35

milling process 36–37, 78

Mint Act 30, 33

mint marks 72

Mint Museum 72

Morgan, J.P 59

Morgan dollar 52

Morris, Robert 26

Morris plan 26–27

mottoes 24, 25, 26, 28, 49, 62

N

National Banking Act 58

National Banking System 49

Native Americans 21, 83

New Orleans mint 43–45

New York 22

nickel 49, 75–76

nitric acid 35

North Carolina 41, 44–45

numismatics 69, 71, 88

O

organizational structure 65–73
  diagram 66–67

P

Page, John 31
pence, British 22
People's Party (see Populist Movement)
pewter 24
Philadelphia 7, 17, 26, 30, 31, 33, 42
Philadelphia mint 30–41, 44, 61, 71, 76, 79, 80, 86
pillar dollars, Spanish 23
Pine Tree Shillings 22
pirates 23
Pittman Act of 1918 62
planchet-cutting process 36
Populist Movement 53–55
pounds, British 22
privateers 23
privately-minted coinage 42
proof coin sets 80

R

Reed, Conrad 41
reeding (see milling)
refining process 35
revolutionary war (see American Revolution)
Rhode Island 22
riddling process 77
Rittenhouse, David 33
Roberts, George E. 59
rolling process 36
Roosevelt, Theodore 58–59, 61–63

S

San Francisco Assay Office 44, 72, 80
San Francisco mint 44, 72
Second Bank of the United States 42–43
seignorage 71, 88
Shaw, Leslie M. 59–60
Sherman Silver Purchase Act of 1890 53

shillings 22
shinplasters 48
silver 22–24, 26, 29, 30, 35, 50–55, 62, 75, 83
silverites 52–55
South, the 18, 41–45, 49–50
Southern Gold Region 41, 43–44
Spain 22–23
Spanish-American War 57
specie 27, 48, 51, 88
stamping process 37–38
State Department (see Department of State)
St. Gaudens, Augustus 61
Subcommittee on Coinage and Consumer Affairs of the House Committee on Banking, Finance, and Urban Affairs 70

T

trade dollars 52
Treasury Department (see Department of the Treasury)

U

uncirculated coin sets 72, 80
United States Bullion Depositories (see Fort Knox)
upsetting process 78

W

wampum 21–22
Washington, George 8, 17, 28, 31, 33, 62
West, the 44–45
West Point Depository 72
World War I 62
World War II 11, 70–71

Z

zinc 70–71, 76